The Sacred Hare

Compiled by
Sharon Zak

ISBN: 978-0-9926648-1-7

First published 2014 by Slippery Jacks Press

Proofreading by Joanne Elliott

Printed for Slippery Jacks by ASKprint.co.uk

Cover: Hare © Rosalie Bottley

Hare

The moon half gone,
and you're dying.

Shot through at the last stand,
your golden head falls
and is caught,
kept as a promise against the dark.

The meadow wraithes
scour the stubbled earth,
But do they find you?
No, for you are gone, dead.

And I,
the sky,
the light,
the waning moon mourns your passing,
standing bereft;
forlorn,
without hope it seems.

The fleeing moon,
shooting over her shoulder on her nightmare career,
sends silver shafts into the heart of dawns growing fire,
but they melt in that moment,
they melt.

This is not the moment in which to kill the growing dark,
and dawns sombre ember consumes the slender shaft,
and swallowing the metaphor,
shortens the day.

by Godfrey Lacks
September night, stubbled field 2013

Harvest Moon © Lisa O'Malley

Goddess in Spring

I feel you my Goddess
As the year slips to Spring
In the warmth of the land
With the sun on my skin

I see you my Goddess
In the light of the dawn
With rain dappled foliage
And cool mists of morn

I hear you my Goddess
In a breath of clear air
With sweet song of birds
And the race of the hare

I sense you my Goddess
As the smoke scented breeze
In soft smell of snowdrops
And awakening trees

I thank you my Goddess
At the dawning of Spring
For the warmth in this land
And the sun on my skin

by Sharon Zak

Eternal Dance © Sharon Zak

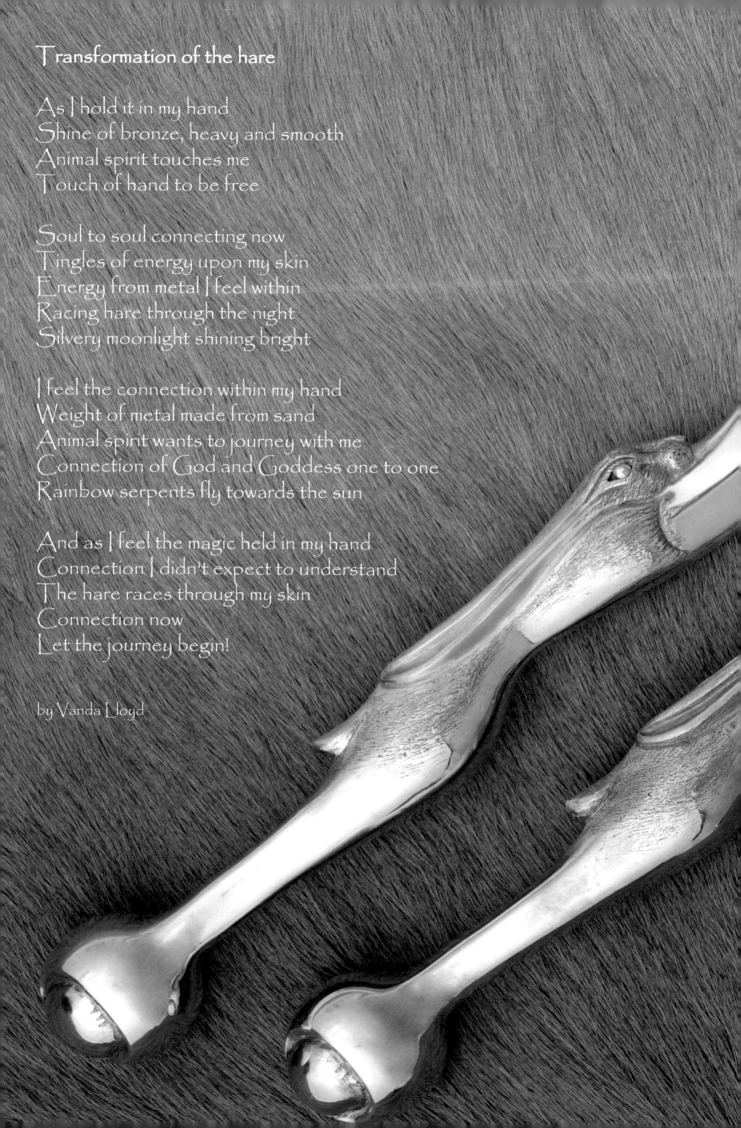

Transformation of the hare

As I hold it in my hand
Shine of bronze, heavy and smooth
Animal spirit touches me
Touch of hand to be free

Soul to soul connecting now
Tingles of energy upon my skin
Energy from metal I feel within
Racing hare through the night
Silvery moonlight shining bright

I feel the connection within my hand
Weight of metal made from sand
Animal spirit wants to journey with me
Connection of God and Goddess one to one
Rainbow serpents fly towards the sun

And as I feel the magic held in my hand
Connection I didn't expect to understand
The hare races through my skin
Connection now
Let the journey begin!

by Vanda Lloyd

Bronze Cunning Hare Athame by Steve Madog

The hare squinted against morning sunlight that gilded the meadow with golden hues. Something felt different today, the light seemed brighter, and the colours more vivid, scents cleaner somehow. She sniffed the air as she surveyed her home looking for what might have caused her to feel this way....
To feel different!

Then she saw it. She blinked hard, it wasn't there yesterday, she'd have seen it surely!

For there in the very centre of the meadow, the one she'd grown up in....
Stood a beautiful tree....

She squinted harder trying to make it out ... puzzling over the sudden appearance of a whole mature tree..... *did they just do that?* she thought to herself, furrowing her brow. She wasn't at all sure they did, normally but today didn't feel normal!

Softly she pottered across the grass to where the tree stood, a growing sense of humbleness making her fur prickle. The little hare looked up into branches high above her, each with their own glistening array of sparkling new leaves drinking in delicious sunlight.

There, under the canopy, the hare realised that she was in the presence of a truly remarkable being.

'Are you a magical tree?' she whispered.

Extract from the forthcoming Hare and Tree Ogham by Sharon Zak

I feel you little hare
as you stand in my shade
your whiskers twitching
sensing
as you try to understand.

Know little hare
I am grateful
that you notice me
at all.

Extract from Hare and Tree Ogham by Sharon Zak

The hare and the magical tree © annie b.

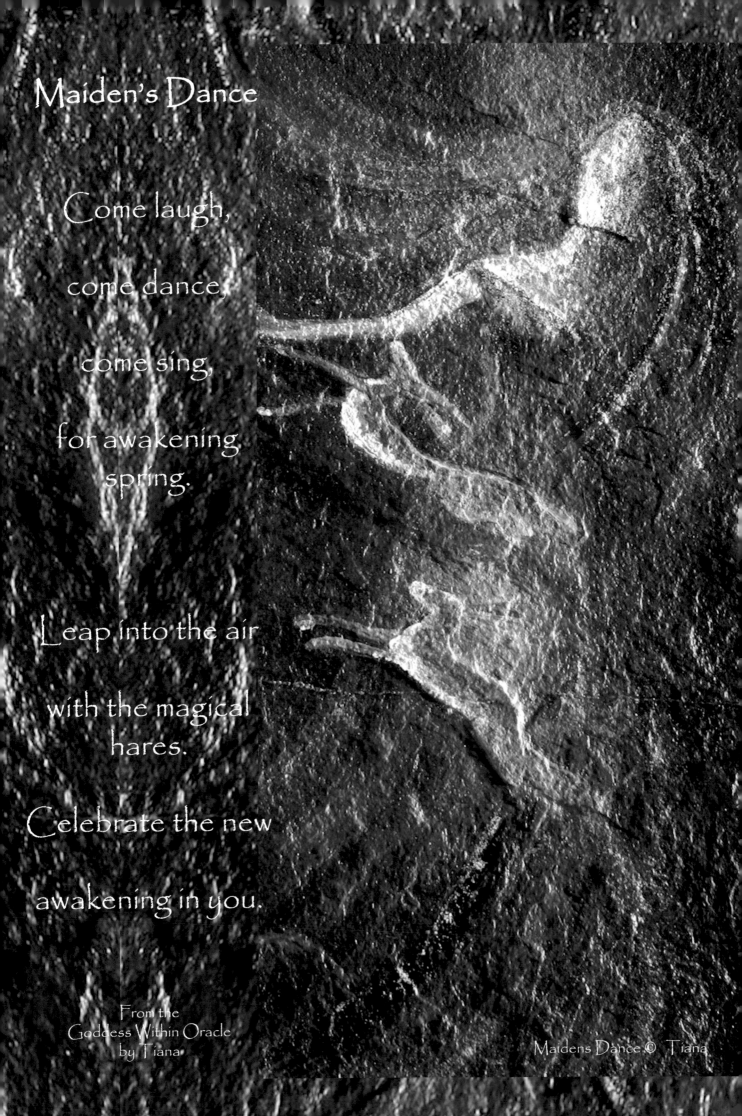

Maiden's Dance

Come laugh,

come dance,

come sing,

for awakening
spring.

Leap into the air

with the magical
hares.

Celebrate the new

awakening in you.

From the
Goddess Within Oracle
by Tiana

Maidens Dance © Tiana

The Brown Hare (Lepus europaeus)

is native to our land, adapted, as it is, to our climate and landscape. But, like many of our non-human natives, it has become increasingly rare.

The brown hare shares its family heritage with the European rabbit but is quite different.

Unlike rabbits they are born above ground, fully furred and with their eyes open. They can grow to 60cm (24 inches) in length and are capable of a staggering 35-45 mph, making them the UK's fastest land mammals. Their speed is their greatest protection against predators with the exception of humans, of course, who still consider this speedy creature to be good sport!

Female hares have three or four litters of leverets a year, which wean at three weeks. Separated from their mothers, these little beings are devilishly difficult to hand-rear with specialist expertise concentrated in the hands of a very small number of exceptional people.

Largely nocturnal, hares spend much of the day alone in a hollow or depression in the ground, a form which serves as a little camouflage. Hares' habitat is predominately arable/grassland, and they thrive in mixed farmland, but they are also found in heathland, woodland and dunes.

Like all other animals hares have a whole range of signals and sounds for communication between themselves and the mother will call to her young using all kinds of guttural sounds.

Hares are most widely known for their boxing behaviours and this is most often seen in spring, it is not 'madness', not at all, but in fact part of both competition and courtship. The bucks will vie for domination while the girls (doe) will willingly beat off an unwanted suitor!

The greatest risk to the hare is agricultural practices in the UK where intensive farming generates desert-like monocultures that fail to accommodate diversity needed for our wildlife. Pressures on food and bio-fuel production will increase so it is up to us to make change happen.

Hare in Gully by Sean Hunter
http://www.seanhunter.co.uk/

Caring for the land, our land, means we also care for the hare that
relies on it. It is their land too.

About the Hare Preservation Trust
The Hare Preservation Trust promotes and encourages all types of
interest in hares, and campaigns to alleviate their persecution for 'sport'
and for changes in agricultural practice.

Contact:
www.hare-preservation-trust.co.uk
PO Box 447, Bridgwater, Somerset, TA6 9GA
Like our Facebook page: Hare Preservation Trust Official
Follow us on Twitter: @HPT_Official

Dreaming The Wild Dance

Pale traveller through the dazzling dark,

Your fleet-foot flight through unseen lands

Is swift and sure to the deep green heart

Of the sleeping seed within her hand

Worlds rise and fall ~ inhale, exhale ~

The quiet wave of Mystery

You know the Whole in your untamed soul

And you are All-That-Is to me.

by Poppy Palin

Dreaming The Wild Dance © Poppy Palin

The ancient standing stone shimmers as the evening
lengthens towards dusk. Warmed by the winter sun it radiates
energy, casting out its message of welcome around it.

Hare feels it and seeking comfort, security and protection
against the cold winter night, she snuggles up against it.
With warm stone against her back, she feels sun energy slowly released.
She knows it will last the night-time and in the morning the sun
would gift more warmth to the land and its inhabitants.

With thoughts of nurture and love filling her mind
she slipped contentedly into dream.
Somewhere in that subliminal space between reality and sleep,
the ancestors came.

The old ones told her of a lifetime long ago, a lullaby that
wrapped itself around her and led her to a time in the past.
Here she saw rock being carved and men telling their stories
through skilled hands. Somehow she was the thread of that connection
snaking through time like a tendril that encircled her as she slept.
Shown through the ancient carvings, hare saw the turning of time
and the importance of the standing stones that were a familiar site
across Albion.

Hare saw a time of honour and devotion to Goddess and the land.
She saw offerings, blessings and praise, ancient practise,
played out in her mind.
And she too felt blessed.

Blessed to have the warmth on her back and the land to sustain her.
Blessed to have the Goddess in her heart and;

Blessed to know the ancestors were but a breath away.

*

And as the morning sun lifted her from dream, she gave thanks.

by Sharon Zak with thoughts by Maria Forrester

Winter Warmth © Maria Forrester

Gather around, come on, get yourselves settled. Yes I know what you saw in the field just then. But quiet now because today I will tell you a new story, created right now, as the breath of Awen ruffles your hair. Wide-eyed little creatures, I see you now as you lift my eyes into smile, for you are the future and this is a story for you. A story to be retold through your lives.... This is a story about the Goddess and the hare.

***

A long time ago when the land was new, when the lush green of spring dappled soft hills under clear blue skies, we meet the young Goddess herself. With the first blush of youth fresh on her skin, she drew herself up scattering flowers like seeds on the wind. Her hair ran in rivulets down through valleys in cascades of pure water to nourish the land and life was so good.

Back then the people knew Her. They honoured Her with thought and deed, she was their Goddess. But change comes swiftly on the wings of time. As the sea receded she saw people turn away, walk away and then, one day they simply failed to recognise Her.

The Goddess wept for their loss, tears splashing hard on rocks as lakes formed around her.

While the people busied themselves with their ever shrinking worlds, scribing hard lines in the earth, the beings of feather and fur came to the Goddess. Long treks across the land in sacred pilgrimage, we call migration. They came and lingered, basking in her abundance, then moved on while time marched forward. Only the hare stayed.

Hare didn't really understand why she was moved so very powerfully, but she made a promise to remain, knowing somehow that she was needed. Knowing that by her sacrifice the darkness would pass again into light as dawn lifted a new day.

The hare nestled against the soft and nurturing body of the Goddess, snuggling down in her form where she felt warm and safe. Time moved forward again in slow, languid waves and still Hare sat. She dared not move, determined to show her dedication to Goddess; and as hunger moved away starvation crept towards her. She wanted nothing for herself, all she knew was that somehow the Goddess needed her. The love of this tiny insignificant creature was needed to bring balance for grief felt by the Goddess.

And as the night gathered around them laying a blanket of frost over the land, the hare slipped into dream, shifting between worlds as the veils parted to accept her. She noticed her fur had turned quite white now and she bent an ear to take a closer look.

Instantly the Goddess saw her and her heart swelled. She gathered up the snow white hare and, holding her close, sang a lullaby of love and devotion. Hare felt the heartbeat of the Mother fill her and almost beyond her perception she heard the song of spring start again. Alive and nourished the hare looked longingly into the eyes of the Goddess and heard Her speak.

'Little soul, as you promised you have stayed with me through my tears, trusting your intuition that balance would return. Today, with the Spring Equinox, you have fulfilled that promise, given your greatest gift. Now, little hare, I have a gift for you.

This is your moment of rebirth!

You will be blessed with great abundance, with the joy of springtime and the blessing of harvest. You will feel me with you always... but more than that, little hare, I give you my heart, gifted to your tender care to carry throughout the year.

You will exist on the very edge of perception, travelling a path between worlds, but oh the joy when you are seen in the world of humankind!

You will forever have the capacity to lift hearts with the rhythm of my own.

The heart you carry in yours.

You are my ambassador, beautiful hare.

You will help call them home.'

***

And the children wept for they had seen the hare, they were home.

Goddess and Hare by Sharon Zak

Hare of Peace © Mia Bradbury

The hare and the butterfly tree © annie b.

Looking up into the dense branches of a venerable old tree the hare saw
something truly magical. High above her head she saw hundreds of butterflies,
all colours and shapes, flitting and flurrying between the boughs.

She wondered what they were doing so high in the foliage
and then she realised, in a moment that
squeezed a tear from her eye,
they were thanking him.

The winter hare and the tree of love © annie b.

Each tiny creature took a moment or two of tenderness, to thank the old tree for his nurture and care, for his company and protection, in their time of transition; he had held their lives to his heart.

And as each tiny creature set out on the next part of their journey, he pulled his leaves into little hearts to show them his love would always remain.

Blessed be

by Sharon Zak

Dance, Dance the circle round
Nice and fast
Round and round

Dance, Dance the circle round
For the Goddess
Of this Land

Words from The Dolmen

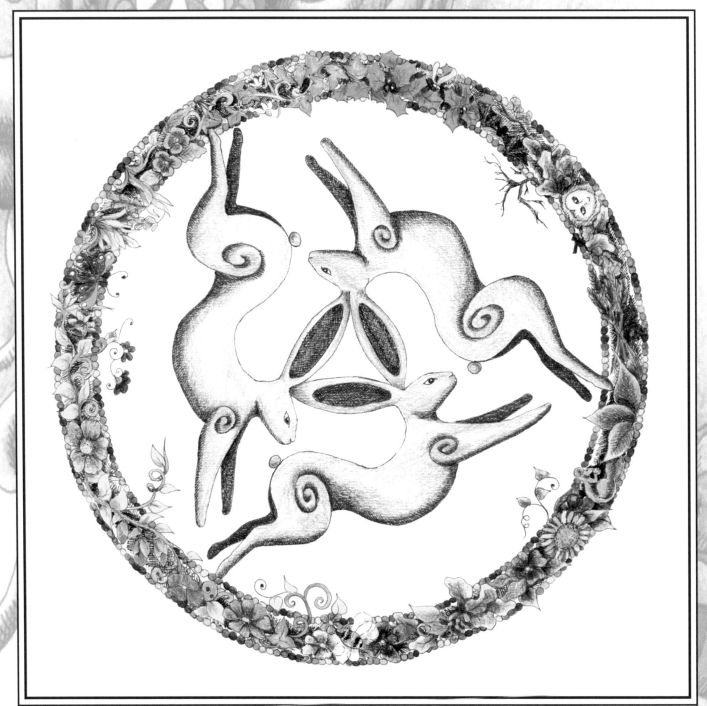

Triple Hare © Gwen Davies

Hare © Gwen Davies

This image grew organically into the story. It is a tale of two worlds.
The land we can see is a glimpse into a secret world of sprites and mythical creatures.
Only a few know of the door which the woman is about to step through,
which is a link between our world and this hidden kingdom.

by Gwen Davies

Magical Mystery

By day I am a shadow that hides in the light,
By darkness a moonbeam that dances the night,
I am the spirit that runs with the Moon,
From Spring Time to harvest, in time
with Earth's tune

I am the spirit of fresh greening fields,
I grow with the year till her harvest she yields

I am the last sheaf bound up with the corn,
The spirit of Earth, forever reborn

I am a shape changer, I change like the year
I fly as the Owl and I run as the Deer

The eggs of the Lapwing are left in my care,
For I am the Mystery and Magic, I am the Hare

So, if you should seek me lying close in my form,
I will run through your dreams from darkness till dawn.

Sharon L. Shute 1998.
Reprinted with honour and deepest respect

Spring Hares © Shari Hills

Hare

Quietly she lays and awaits the dusk, in a field now graced with green,
She softly breathes. The catkins stir. Only by the white owl she is seen.
Her eyes are wild and amber, her fur brown and a-glow with red,
Oh how she does enchant me! My mind from me has fled.

The wind does bellow and it does blow. The hedgerow along she races,
Into the air she twists and turns as her freedom she embraces,
She crouches in the plough's deep furrow, transfixed by the moon's
bright ring,
Light and darkness in the balance is held on this equinox of spring.

In the silver shadows I watch her pass, but her form does trick my eye,
Her silhouette it leaps and bounds, then vanishes into the sky,
And the dervish whirl of autumn's fall is all that now remains,
As the scarlet flames of sundown, into darkness slowly wanes...

At the birth of a new March dawn, from an oak, the blackbird sings,
And the fair haze of this morning, a figure it now brings,
For in the mist a creature moves; she frolics, frisks through the air.
Along the hedgerow once more does race, the elusive, magical hare!

by Rose Blakeley

www.roseblakeley.moonfruit.com

Hara © Rose Blakeley

I wait for you now
Breath bated, pulled in
And spring gathers pace
And the fields turn to green

I remember you now
From the year here before
As I pull up my chair
To the window once more

My wheels barely creak
As I slide into place
Looking out to the land
My heart in a race

I know when I see you
My spirits will soar
You'll set my heart free
When I join you once more

And today as I wait
For that first precious glance
I know that as much
I am part of your dance

by Sharon Zak

Sunset House © Tamsin Abbott

One air, our breath
One land, our home

The Witch-Hare

My pulse it pounds and paces. Across the valley slopes I streak,
Then my curious disappearance creates an air of some mystique,
For fast am I, but also sly; the huntsman I elude with ease
And all that's found by the frustrated hounds is a whisper in the trees.

The coast is close; the alluring salt-breeze entices me to the sea,
But you sailors off to fare the waves, stay away must I from thee!
For in your minds, you fear that I can summon a storm or gale,
So peace I grant thee, and from the ocean's view I merrily turn my tail.

Mischief inspirits me as the lush wheat sighs. At the dairy I linger and laze,
A small sip of milk is all I require, but the maids seem unsettled and dazed.
I think I must leave...for what's that I hear? A strange affect, I have on some.
For away as I scamper, then echoes the sound, of a chanting...*come, butter, come!*

I gambol and groom in the meadow sweet. The skylark elates with its song,
High in its kingdom of azure blue, with the swallows, where they belong.
Motley, silk flowers cushion my way; in the warm grass they interweave.
I stretch my long limbs, as the great sun dips, relishing this Midsummer's Eve.

Into the lantern-lit town, quietly I slip. Garlands embellish each door,
To evade the festive masquerades, the old inn's window, I stand here before
And I hear strange tales, told around the fire, of a witch, one crooked and grey,
Who lives alone, but is never seen. A perplexing figure this yarn does portray.

Some say she lives on the wide valley slopes; can transform herself into a hare.
She tricks and bamboozles for her own amusement, so gentle folk, please be beware!
I do not wish to scare or harm, a little fun, now and then, is my aim,
Once more I must go, for if I am caught, I'll be trapped, and me they will maim.

My pulse it pounds and paces. Across the verdant slopes I speed,
But in my heart this time is joy, for to my home I now recede,
Oh in the morning I'll be old, for the spell from me will wear
And till I return, no longer I'll be, a beautiful, wild, brown hare.

by Rose Blakeley

Hare © Mary Walton

If you are lucky enough, gentle enough, aware enough, you may see hares boxing in the fields, what a gift that would be. For instead of a beast that shares its genes with the familiar and docile rabbit, the hare is quite different. Rather than a domesticated creature we see a strikingly independent being that carries with it the weight of folklore, mythology and tradition that spans eons.

We revered these magnificent creatures in the UK and we were not alone for the hare weaves her way through our psyche in the company of the moon, linked to the Goddess both in her lunar form and as the White Goddess of the land.

Ancient animistic beliefs that pervade human cultures saw the hare as one of a pantheon of beings that could guide and inform our future well-being, ensure our survival even.

Companion to the Goddess Eostre the hare represents love, life, fertility and growth and was associated not only with the moon but with the coming of dawn and of death and rebirth.

There is a powerful mythology linking hares to shape-shifting and this is particularly associated with women. Eostre herself was believed to change into a hare at the full moon and many tales tell of this remarkable ability. Boudicca was said to have taken a hare into battle with her to ensure victory and it was said to have screamed like a girl from beneath her cloak.

Such was the strength of belief in the hare that it could not be repressed. Instead it was subsumed into the new Christian religion that swept pagan lands and is still seen in Christian settings today though few people are aware of its journey to this place.

And now, as we consider the way our ancestors and our lives are entwined with the hare, how we bury our faces in its thick fur, breathing in the scent of this divine and sacred being, we know that we share, with them, our future.

by Sharon Zak
(Inspired by alll those who have written before me)

Moon Dancers © Becky Munting

Spirit Hare

Totem of the Divine

Cast in Full Moonlight

As a Reflection

Of the Elements

Captured

In Time

by Sharon Zak

Pyrographed hare platter on wooden plate © Paula McFadyen

My hare spirit totem in full moon reflection.
The process corporates earth, air, fire and water - and of course spirit!

Hare in the Making - Sculpture © Paula McFadyen

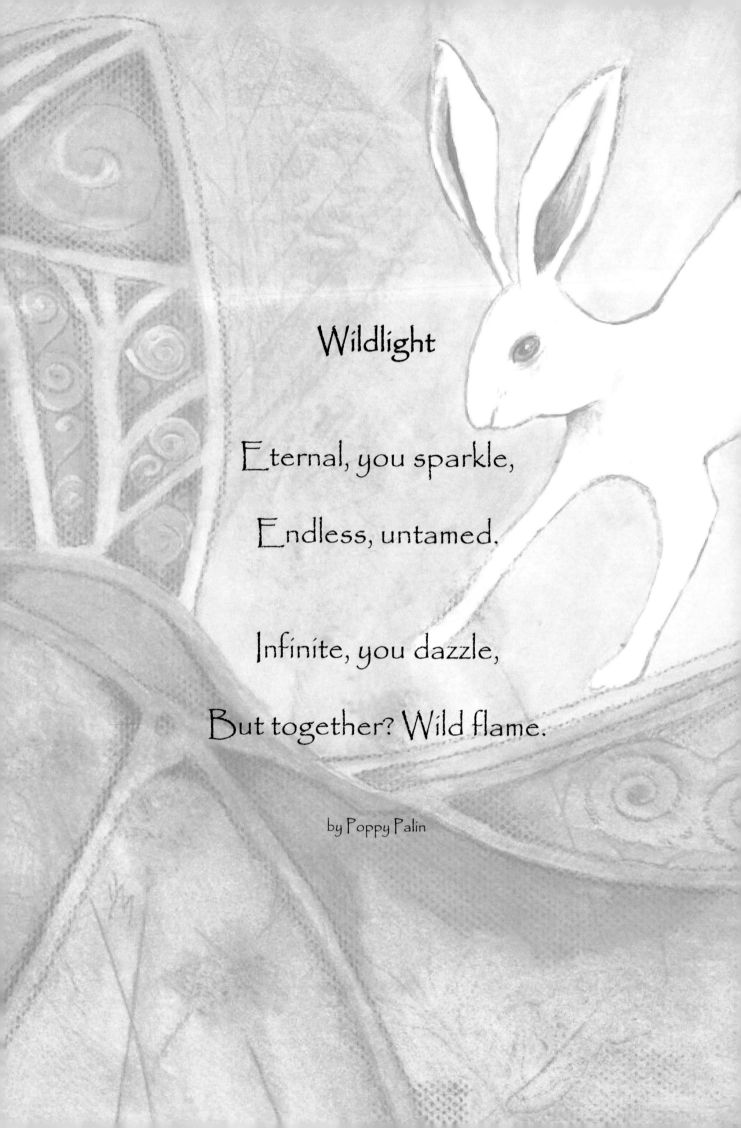

Wildlight

Eternal, you sparkle,

Endless, untamed.

Infinite, you dazzle,

But together? Wild flame.

by Poppy Palin

Hare with Standing Stones © Maria Forrester

After Yeats 'Collar Bone of the Hare'

Treading a path of moonlight
each pebble shaped by sea's
smoothings, the airs
abrading touch ,
shadows sharp
dip down before our feet.

We follow the hare
stepping into her
sleight of foot
patterns.
They fill with lunar
silver light and we
sharpen our gaze
to peer through Moons
hazey maskings to
find our footings.
Down through grasses,
thrift, pinks , mallows all
colours stolen by the night.
Down, down
to the waters
through the goddess light.

Slip,slip our heavy
earthen forms
to dip shapeless
beneath the sea,
caress the broidered silks
of swaying greens
caught, suspended
as in a sea- glass.

See the waters lap
at the fine,worn
collar bone ....
transparent now but
only peer through
the piercing, meet
Yeats startled
blue gaze.
Watch as the Goddess
reconstructs the precious
hare, gifts her life .

She flies free, dissolved
softened, released
in shards of Light,
dancing to laughter that
shines as music
across the quiet
glistening
water.

by Tina Burnett

Under a Pale Moon © Lisa O'Malley

Brigid Bright

I put my ear close to the Earth
on this cold Imbolc day
to hear Bright brigid's songs.

she sings of Moon's supernal , starlit rites
dance of the hare on wild spring nights
of how she curls alone,
against the sky
in secret
hollow
spaces.
She sings of owl
as she glides in silent flight,
to watch
from hidden
places.

Cold Imbolc Day © Christine Burnett

She calls the dance of the holy bees
as they fly their crazy, blissful ways
scrawls water patterns in the sand
at oceans's edge
while balancing
the heave and heft of seas.

Standing at the crux
of all the days
With bowl and slender
willow wand
She weaves her sacred songs
and treads the curve
of meadow lands
to walk the ancient leys.

These secret spirit tracks
that thread the Earth around
with ancient wisdom's pulse
Her sacred, joyful sound.

by Christine Burnett

The Meadow Lands © Christine Burnett

I Know

I know you see me in the meadows of your mind

As spring approaches and hope, alive, lifts spirits into song

I know you hear me in the beating of your heart

As we walk across sacred land, rhythms entwined

I know you feel me in the depths of your soul

As we bathe, blessed, in moonlight divine

I know you recognise the song I sing

You know I sing for the land

And my Spirit sings

for you.

by Sharon Zak

Golden Hares © Shari Hills

Hare

I see the madness in your eye;
a mirror,
I recognise the terror.

Not knowing,
but hearing the calling,
I follow,
follow,
and here I stand,

The moon bright in my eye,
waiting your command.

by Godfrey Lacks
Alban Elfed 2013

I Love You But It's Time To Leave

You move between the lines,

Fleeting on margins, sleek shadow-seeker,

Always skirting, never waiting,

Sloping, loping, skittering

Thistledown silent, lean and light,

You leap to kiss the wind.

My feet shift stones and so you freeze

Twixt worlds you meet my gaze

Held for dancing eternity, you and I,

Heartbeat wild-drumming infinity

At the edgelands, beyond all reason,

Hung with twilight, wood-smoke and memory.

I yearn, a tear falls,

You slip away.

by Poppy Palin

I Love You But it's Time To Leave © Poppy Palin

I saw her as I drove past
Too fast
The glimpse, bolt upright
in a golden drift of dandelions
back rod straight
to the tip of her ears
in a perfect line
eyes wide
alert

I left my awareness with her
in a momentary pause
that lasted an age

I looked
Took her in
Her sleek lines
And felt the beauty
Of this wild, vibrant creature

I marvelled that she allowed me
This moment of connection
Across time
Between species

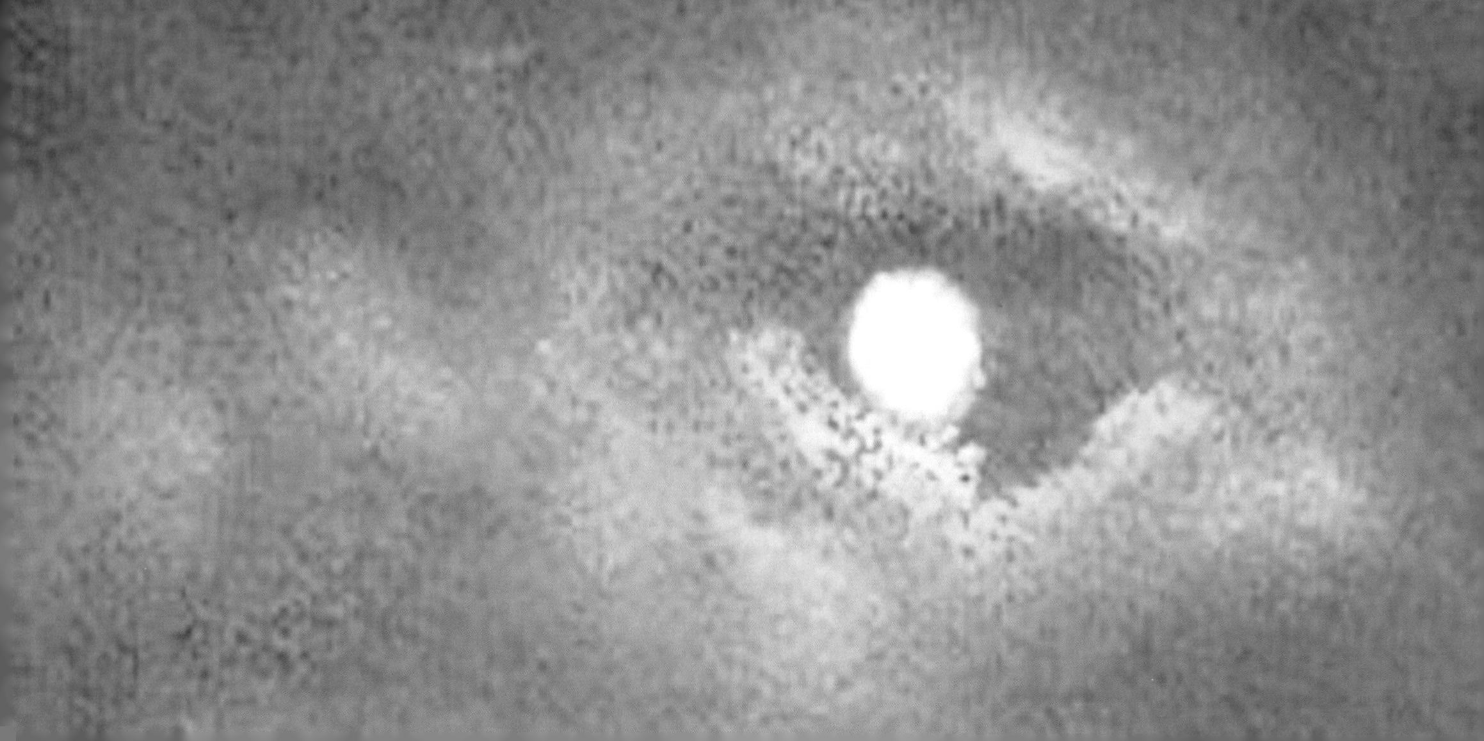

And I wondered
What she thought
Of me.

by Sharon Zak

Watchers Moon © Gary Anderson

So Said the Hare...

In silence I see my Beloved and bathe in her soft, dewy glow.

Oh what mysteries has she revealed to me;
what songs has she taught to my soul.

Her sweet, changing face takes me away to a time that is no time,
and yet this time it is; to a land that is no land, and yet this same land it is.

Under her light I feel the pulse of the earth
and surrender to the caress of the wind.

I hear the veins of life,
flowing over the grass,
running with the river,
flourishing on the trees.

My Beloved needs not to call me,
for my sight is forever on her.

And under her pale rays I stand still,
and let my heart be a beacon

between Heaven and Earth.

by Karem Barratt

Moongazing Hare 2 © Lauren Isherwood

Carry me
Through
This field of stars

Lead me
Onwards

In my imagination

To a world
of Adventure
and
Opportunity

by Sharon Zak

Moongazing Hare © Jan Fowler

Gentle hare beneath the glowing moon,
totem spirit basking in the light.

Stay awhile, don't leave too soon,
offer guidance this magic night.

Wait with me in peaceful reverence
and guide me on,
with balance and love in my heart.

Hare of Healing © Mia Bradbury

You are the sacred bringer
of abundance and hope.

Beyond this beautiful night
of twinkling stars lost in time,
may I wake
rejuvenated
and reborn.

by Mia Bradbury

Hare of Love © Mia Bradbury

I sleep beside the ancient hills
Nestled within this hallowed landscape .

One that inspired the bard to magic and myth.
Amongst the tales of dragon lines that call out loud to the dowsers rod.

I lay gently between those hazy veils of mystic and delight
where the Fae claim the dawn.

Walking the land, leaving footprints as they go, to discover, if you
know how to look

Here lie the stories told in your youth remembered and recalled.
In fables embellished in the telling with moral fortitude
The gift of fear in exchange for your good behaviour

Then we tell of those of the women who lived on the land
accused, convicted, hanged in a wave of superstitious nonsense.

That took their essence and passed it from them into us
Where they remain chronicled to this day a reminder of the past

And tonight while I sleep I will keep having dreams
While the Fae walk the land and the dragons still sleep.

I will dream a new song as the darkness descends
Of enchantment and magic gifted back to the land.

That will pass, unnoticed.

From me on to you.

by Sharon Zak

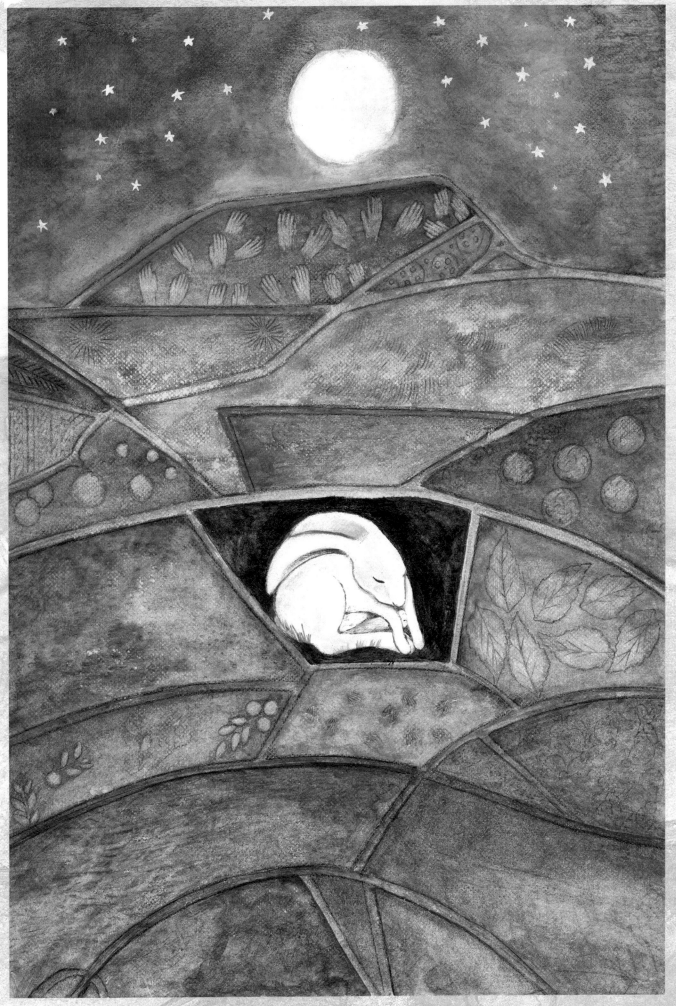

Pendle Hare © Maria Forrester

Here is Lughnasadh,
poised at the opposite point
in the sacred wheel of the year, from Beltaine,
it heralds the first harvest.

Product of an annual union of
God and Goddess,
Sun King and Mother Earth,
this is a time of gathering and celebration
for preparation for the dark to come.

With garlands of meadowsweet, marigold and mint
we bake Lammas bread to gift and share,
kneeded with love, hope and courage
decorated with ribbon and a few ears of corn,
spreading the abundance we feel in our lives.

Reaping what we have sewn in the year,
we take time to give thanks for all those gifts.
Gathering seed, energy, sustenance, hope
for the future we know that whatever we face today,
abundance will come again.

But just as important as out stories and myths
are our own thoughts and feelings for this time of the year.

What does it mean to you?

What are the stories you weave for yourself?

Write in here your own tale, weave it
around the words on the page and gather
the energy of Lughnasadh
for yourself.

by Sharon Zak

Hare!

September,
You golden beauty;
Long shanks of corn gold hair
laid out in tresses,

that falls and flows
from shoulder to back

and caresses,
distant hills,
and blesses

the dark hounds
at your heels.

by Godfrey Lacks

Luna Moon Hare at Lammas © Wendy Andrew

Poppy heads and teasels wave softly
as autumn brushes them with its golden gloved hand.

Pregnant with seed they sense the time has come,
the moment of release;
that wisest of times when we give back
what has been borrowed from the land.

The hare leaps between them
scattering hope in her wake,
knowing that the cycle
of life, death and rebirth
will turn
as fertile soil
received her gifts.

And then,
as a warm sun kisses their nodding heads,
a sparkling cloud of goldfinches
receive their own
abundant blessing.

And the wheel
turns

by Sharon Zak

Leaping Hares © Shari Hills

We sat together on a little toy of a train, small guage, that wove its way through the grounds of the park. It was a regular journey cast into relief by child and his love of trains. It was a much loved treat for my Grandson and me, time to be and to be together.

We'd taken it in turns his father and I, to travel the route and share his joy. Each of us delighting in his gleeful chatter as the train pottered along at a snail's pace.

On this day, as hot spring sunshine warmed us, the driver simply pointed. Hushed into silence we all followed his line, and there, lounging full stretch in the sun, was a magnificent hare. Warming his own winter weary bones, his elegant body, lean and fit, long limbs outstretched in his repose.

I can't describe how that fleeting glimpse made me feel.. elated comes close. Oh! the excitement that I felt in that precious experience, that moment of sharing. I felt my soul lifted into song, singing for the joy of life and the gift of this magical beast; joy that remains as I tell the tale.

My son went to look too, but, having relaxed in a lovely sun kissed patch of grass all day, the hare had gone.

This was a magical moment.

Just for B and me.

For T and B by Sharon Zak

Heart of the Meadow © Sara Ferris

Guardian spirits of this land
Spirits of this place
We call upon your gentle wisdom
to help us connect to the land of the old
To Albion fair, the land of our ancestors.
Help us to treasure Her
to experience Her gifts

Guardian spirits of this land
Spirits of this place
We call upon your gentle wisdom
to help us connect to the land of the old
To Albion fair, the land of our ancestors.
Help us to treasure Her
to experience Her gifts

Help us find the strength and the voice
to protect our forests and streams
help us to choose well
and to make change with our decisions
with our hearts and our actions.

Help us to guard our belovid Earth

So may it be

by Sharon Zak

Guardians © Erica Hemming

Wide-eyed she stared,
unable to move,
such was her excitement.

"Tell me about Her?"
The hare whispered into badger's delicate old ear.

Her heart was filled to the brim
with the extraordinary beauty of
what she saw hanging there in the sky.

The old badger smiled,
he too was in awe
but he was a wise old soul,
he knew.

"What do you feel?"
he asked softly.

The sound of his voice seemed to travel
right through hare's fur,
into her very being.

Like a key,
it opened her up
to the profound experience
of this night.

Before she could respond,
long before her thoughts gathered
and began to coalesce,
she began to feel.

And the enchantment of
Divine Light
washed over her.

by Sharon Zak

Hare and Badger © Jan Fowler

I look to you Eostre, Moon Goddess, White Goddess, Moon Mother
Bright Moon bathing in your blessed light
Giving thanks for your wandering spirit
In the depths of this night

by Sharon Zak

Moon Gazing Hare © Jan Fowler

Spring stirs
Pushing snowdrops into drift
To lift
And awaken our spirit
Washing winter from our skin

by Sharon Zak

Imbolc Hare © Jan Fowler

The Lookouts © Becky Munting

Red Ball © Becky Munting

The Farmer and the Hare

Old brown hare sat on her form
happy in the evening sun,
one ear up, one ear down
velvet nose twitching, twitching.

Farmer comes to fetch the cows
happy in the evening sun,
one foot forward, other foot forward
calling the cows, calling.

Old brown hare settles low
sinking like the evening sun,
one breath in, one breath out
ready for the running, running.

Farmer comes on ever closer
circling in the evening sun,
one breath in, one breath out
long shadow growing.

Old Puss jumps, a mighty leap
galloping in the evening sun,
front legs bounding, back legs bounding
Farmer watches as she goes, smiling, smiling.

by Stuart Taylor

Shari Hills

Sunset Hare © Shari Hills

Grandmother Cry

I hear you Grandmother
Your cry carries across the fields
Pulling me from my home
Leading me out of my perfect dream
As spring softens the land to green
And the Sun King kisses my face
I hear your sorrow, feel your pain.

With guns crooked in old Barbour green
They file past my farm cottage
Day in, day out
Wearing smiles of satisfaction
With blood dripping from calloused hands.

And in the distance, unheard by them
You call out your lament for the young ones
Their wisdom, their intuition, yet to mature
These were the ones who leapt into the light
Revealed themselves
Manifest in the reality of men.

And then, sharp sound, left broken bone
And blood returned to the land
A life claimed, left unclaimed
In that moment, outside the dream
I join the Grandmother and cry.

by Sharon Zak

Hares © Martin Herbert

The Sacred Hare – Down-Under

What is this? Where am I?
Everything is all topsy turvey.
I've been transported somewhere far away from home.
Have I landed Down-Under in Australia?

When I look around me I see strange trees.
My nose twitches and picks up the scent of eucalyptus.
The earth is giving off a sunburnt odour
While the grasses are all dry and brown

Hey! There's a kangaroo hopping by.
I call out "Hello", and he responds "G'day Mate".
In the distance I can hear the strange laugh of the kookaburra
While above, the chattering of parrots in the tree tops.

The sun is fiercely beating down, searing my skin.
Oh! My furry coat is so hot and sweaty.
Blissfully, I espy a shady grass tree where I can rest
'til the cool of sunset draws near.

Resting, I muse awhile, pondering my fate.
Back in England we were approaching the Spring Equinox
But here! This is not the same season I am sure
Maybe it's their Autumn Equinox.

Whatever the season, it is a time of balance
with equal hours of day and night.
Where the birth of our Blessed Moon begins
Progressing, for equal time, through the enchanted night
To fade away to death at dawn.

Night has come to me in all its glory
With the full moon shining above.
I am a tad scared in this strange land
But the Moon Goddess surely watches over me.

While I secretly bask in the moonlight
The night swiftly passes by.

Original Hare © Lauren Isherwood

My intuition clicks in – I know this is the start
of my journey, my new life down-under.

The Southern Hemisphere is similar to the North
Just the dates of the seasons differ
There is a change to, during Ceremonies
One's path follows an anticlockwise direction.

Where ever I may be
I am still "The Sacred Hare"
Meeting my Goddess of the Moon
For all eternity.

by Yvonne Hortin

My Final Leap

You beat me up, beat me out in the open and I run

Greyhound bitch breath hard against my skin

Fur crawling

But my spirit-self watches from the side lines

Taking in death, my death, your pleasure

Taking in the puny and pathetic, the self-righteous
and sanctimonious

For the mindless cruelty you so relish

Disgust creeps and I turn it into pity

I know my Goddess watches with me

As you tear flesh from bone

I turn way, tearful for your species

I reach for Her hand

and take my final leap

by Sharon Zak

The Leap Into Ancestry © Sharon Zak

Moon Lullaby

I am the Silver Phoenix that lives, dies and comes to be again,
forever mirrored on the enamoured hare's eyes .

I am unchanged but never the same.

Each of you, children, are reflections of mine.

From the moment of awakening to the closing of the lids,
your days are a likeness of my movements, changes, wanes, waxes,
darkness and sudden light that clarifies it all.

Be brave my daughter, in your inner journey and you shall
reach the realms of vision, where intuition and inspiration
come together as one.

Be daring, my son, and go through the hurricane of bewilderment.
At its centre you shall find peace and the answer
to your heart's uncertainties.

Everything changes my children, yet remains the same.

My cycles are reminders of the phases we must go through
to grow and fulfil ourselves.

I am the Heavenly Mistress that sings lullabies to your
blood and makes it rise with the power of the tides.
Flow with me and dance the secrets of life
with each shake of your hips.

Travel with me to the all possible futures.
Sigh with me.
Place in me your doubts and let them ripe to truths in the soil your dreams.

I am Juliet's moon, and Plato's, Newton's and Copernicus'.
Love poems have been written under my light as well as Gospels.
Flow with me and let's dance together to the Universe's reverie.

by Karem Barratt

Havergate Hare © Alexi Frances

You dreamed me
into existence

You woman!

You witch!

With your beauty
and guile

Your loving smile

With your nurturing soul
and your passionate goal

You called to me
as your wild side

And I came as your foil
From rich soil

I came as your sister
As mother
As friend

For the love of all existance

And I stand now beside
the man of the wood

As Lady of the Land
and the Lord of Green

by Sharon Zak

Hare © Rosalie Bottley

I feel the spirit of the hare but none so much as when I'm at work on the maternity unit. I'm surrounded by the high pitched cries of new lives just beginning and other lives being changed forever. Dealing with it every day, seeing perhaps friends and family having children around us or even the television now airing documentary style programmes on birth, it's easy to forget what a truly magical process of bringing a new being into the world is. And with all our modern day technology and procedure it's easy to miss part of our magical human experience.

Have you ever had the privilege of witnessing a birth or a labour? I have. Maybe some of you reading this have too? If you have it's likely it was an unforgettable experience!
Labour is one of the most spectacular windows through which to view us humans in our most natural and primitive state. The body takes over entirely, instinct comes to the forefront and societies expectations completely drop away causing us to do what we must to bring forth new life. A woman may go completely inside of herself, bringing forward strength, an unwavering focus, power and determination that she may not have even known she had. We become the human animal. I see us humans delivering our young with much similarity as the hare on the fields delivers its leverets. At that time mobile phones, fashion, cars, money...mean absolutely nothing. Right in that moment of time, our bodies, our babies, our family and love are all that matters.

Once our child has arrived, the hares' connection with new beginnings, life, infinity and eternity remain with us, embodied in the new life that has entered the world. We may ask ourselves what changes, and impact, might this person bring about? The mother now starts a new chapter in her life as parents, guardian, guide and protector all bound together with the energy of eternal and unconditional love.

If we take a moment to step back, I see the circle of the hares in an unbreakable motif. As with all nature... this cycle will continue, the spirit of the hare will always be with us.

by Anna Newberry

Fruitful Hares © Shari Hills

Come to me children
Suckle, take sustenance
Fill yourselves with my love
For I give willingly
and I am
Never
Far from you

by Sharon Zak

Butterfly Hare © Shari Hills

'I wish I could fly' whispered the hare to no one in particular as she watched the butterfly
settle before her. And to her surpise the fragile creature spoke.

'Imagine yourself racing acorss the buttercup meadows. Leaping in long grass that sways
in the summer breeze. Think back, that's right. Look at what you can do, what you can
achieve all by yourself. You are capable of so much little hare.
For when you run so very fast, when your
heart races, when nothing else matters,
you do fly.'

by Sharon Zak

Oh, Little Ghost

Swimming the surging tide of night,

Riding the ripples of dancing light,

Breaking on shores beyond our sight

In indigo pools deep glimmering.

Oh, whispering ghost of flickering white,

Pale hare rising, burning bright,

On waves of longing, lunar sprite

With a hidden gold heart glittering.

Dark is the sea and the human plight,

Shadowed is the moon and our delight,

Silvered wing and a prayer take flight,

Last singing seed starts shimmering.

by Poppy Palin

The Singing Seed © Poppy Palin

Prayer to the Triple Mother

Mother of the Earth, lady of the jungles and the mountains;
giver of harvests and maker of deserts,
be the dust under my feet and the cool water that quenches my thirst;
whisper to me in the voice of the wind and wave hello with the
gentle quiver of flowers along my way;
make me feel welcome with your aromas of fresh bread
and thawed the cold from my bones with the warmth of your hearth.

Mother of the skies, womb of comets and stars,
colour my eyes with dreams and my spirit with rainbows;
inspire me, in your cosmic silence, beauty born out of your essence and
answer the questions of my soul with the glow of the full moon.

Mother of Love, seated between the pillars of eternity:
call me to the temple of your mysteries and potentials, to your lotus throne,
to your mantle of light, to that paradise found in the middle of my heart,
and as I walk to the new beginnings, to the Summer Lands,
on the Other Side, hold me, as if I were a babe,
and with a tiny voice, tell me the truths of the Universe,
of Death and Life.

Hug me against your bosom Mother of mine,
oh Maiden, oh Mother, oh Crone,
and with your song,
cover me with compassion,
grant me courage
and give me hope.

by Karem Barratt

Good Hare Days © Shari Hills

The Hare

Until I moved to Ireland I had never seen a hare in real life but now in the Spring, if I am lucky they come and play in my garden. Sometimes they are alone, sometimes they come in pairs but always they fascinate me.

A few years ago with no idea why I was buying it I become the happy owner of a tiny silver Hare charm. Like many things I have around me I just trusted my instincts and bought it even though I had no idea why I was buying it nor what I would do with it.

Then during my first year working on the Bard level of the OBOD I came across Hare once again and reading about the symbolism of Hare I began to understand why I had been drawn to buy one. I love the sense that Hare brings luck, fertility and healing but more than anything it is the idea of Hare being associated with rebirth that I am drawn to.

As a healer the sense of being reborn is always with me whether I am working on myself or clients, the thought that each moment as we heal we can be born anew. As a shamanic healer, death and rebirth are a constant for me contained in many of my rituals and also in some of my shamanic journeying.

Within life, like everyone, I move through cycles, I am all too aware of some and others work away unseen but with all of them I know I will reach a point where something has to die, to be let go of and that if I can do this, let go of the past, or of something that no longer serves me, then I am creating space for something new to come in, again a form of rebirth.

There is no fear of this just joy in knowing I can be reborn over and over again. Now that I know, I carry Hare with me and that Hare can assist me, I know I have found a new talisman and maybe even a guide.

Due to this I decided I would journey to meet the spirit of Hare and see what I could learn directly from it:

Here I am standing in a dip in the ground, soft rolling land around me. I hear in my mind the word 'dell' and instinctively know that where I am standing is in fact a dell. I feel the soft springy grass beneath my feet and after standing enjoying the sensation for a time I let my feet lead me down the slope.

As I move my footsteps slow and I become aware of movement in front of me. Hare appears from nowhere, materialising a short distance ahead of where I am now frozen to the spot. As I watch Hare stands up on its hind legs, paws raised, and begins to shadow box.

All at once I understand why Hare has come now and what it is showing me. It becomes clear that it is telling me to stop fighting my own shadow, that this is a waste of time and energy. It is far better to acknowledge and accept my shadow side, heal what I can at this time and coexist with what I cannot, rather than to try and fight it or 'box' it in attempt to keep it under control, locked away.

As this understanding coalesces Hare drops its stance and hops off up the slope opposite and away. I am left feeling immensely grateful that Hare has come to me and shared this insight. I know there are many more insights to be learnt from Hare, much, much more that it can teach me and I know that I am open to learning whatever it can share. My new awareness feels like a rebirth and the freedom that it brings feels wonderful.

by Yvonne Ryves
Author of Shaman Pathways Web of Life, shamanic and energy healer and OBOD Bard.

WhiteHare at Sunset © Maria Forrester

Rest

Go within

and rest

awhile.

Nurture
that within.

From the
Goddess Within Oracle
by Tiana

the sickles fall
cutting ears of wheat
in this glorious heat
the Sun and spirits call

he pours the mead
to bless the land
and initiate the feast

abundance it is indeed
could he more demand?
he sings of joy at least

one fleeing hare
is being cheered
by the working folk

this ain't no joke
the acre is bare
and fall is no longer feared

by Hennie van Geel

Moon Gazing Hare 1 © Lauren Isherwood

Balance and Intution

Moon and Night

Promise and Fullfilment

Dawn and Bright

Shapeshifting

Between worlds

Leap into consciousness

Excitement of rebirth

Fertility and Abundant

Willing release

Change

Feminine

Wild and free

Essence of nature

Hope for the land

Hope for you

Are these the things I mean?

collected by Sharon Zak

Notice Me

Do you make fun of me?
Mock me with caricature
Denigrate me with fluffy tails and idiot tales?
Forgetting your heritage
Turning from your own song
As you dance to that of another?

I ask, notice me now
As companion and messenger
As the bringer of song and the image of spring
Watch me leap in the dawn with the quickening spirit
Alive with the heartbeat of the land

Know me again as my life plays out with yours.
As our destinies entwine
Across time
As we chase, rush and spin through the year

Notice me as you tear up the land
While you fracture Her body and poison Her rain
Letting them come for profit and gain
Their short term plan and their long term aim

Notice me
When I'm gone

by Sharon Zak

Hare and Duchy Trees 1 © Shari Hills

February

Why Hare,
there you are,
there!

Well, this is the other side of the coin;
when I remember Septembers herbal warmth,
rising and dizzying my senses,
and now I stand stamping and blowing
on this iron hard earth,
still clad with snow.

And there's you;
loping away across freshly combed and harrowed soil,
You can't wait for it to sprout can you?
What a gamble;
the green shoots for your young?
Why no,
for you are Hare!

by Godfrey Lacks
Imbolc 2013

Boxing Hares © Tamsin Abbott

Sacred Hare-Gift From The Moon

Through bramble and fern, softly she hops
Across farmland and furrow avoiding farmer's shots.
At twilight she's twitching; waiting for me,
To follow on a journey, together we flee.
I stumble and tumble as we race along free,
I become her and she becomes me.

A pathway made, through the warming earths flowers,
Wood anemone, primrose, the wild garlics power.
The scents of the woodland leading us on,
An enchanted space; where the fairies sing their song.
The promise of bluebell and wild Orchid to come,
But dusk is descending and it's time to move on.

Light and quick she scampers through fading light,
Glimpses of grey and white in the night.
A silvery moon and starlight bright,
A secret knowledge, she'll teach me this night.
Where magic and mystery; just out of sight,
Will all become clear when she shines her bright light.

Sacred Hare gift from the moon,
A transforming light after winter's gloom.
Bubbling energy rising up, creativity, love and luck
Lightening, lifting we follow along,
All is made new, in a sweet spring song.

by Joanne Elliott

She appears
like magic
emerging from your dream
into reality
for the briefest
of moments

before
vanishing
as quickly
as she came

by Sharon Zak

Fern Hare © Shari Hills

Fiery Hare

I held you in your raw form
Before you were polished
Before you shone and showed all of you
All your details and features
I held you

,And I still found you beautiful
I felt the fire of spirit coming from within you
Saw the spark of the flame released in your breath
Watched you bounding over the land
On your journey, my journey

I touched you, hands tingling with your energy
Felt the shapes of being within you
Moonlight hare, raw like the moon
Moonlight power racing through you
Heard you call
Come – journey now with me

by Vanda Lloyd

Bronze Cunning Hare Athame by Steve Madog

With love and thanks to all the amazingly generous people who gave so willingly for this book to be created.
What an incredible gift you have given the world. Blessed be.

Tamsin Abbott – I live in rural east Herefordshire with my husband, Mike and our two children. Whilst I am working in my studio making stained glass Mike is running green woodwork courses in a nearby woodland, or working at home, writing or chair making. We have self published one book together (he wrote it and I illustrated it) and it is now in its third print run. (Check out www.living-wood.co.uk for more information about this and Mike's green wood-working courses.)

Long before I met Mike I completed a degree in English literature at Stirling University (1985 -1989) where I specialised in medieval literature. I was drawn to Stirling by the landscape and the wildness of the mountains and hills. I was not disappointed and was surrounded by a suitable back-drop for the subject I was studying. My love of the language and stories of medieval literature was enhanced by the fact that much of the research material I was reading was illustrated with paintings and simple woodcuts of the period. I became immersed in a magical world of romance, strange words and naïve but arresting images, and it was not long before I began to paint and write for pleasure as well as working for the degree.

Gary Anderson – Gary was born, and grew up in Ayrshire on the West coast of Scotland. He now lives on an estate in South Ayrshire with his partner, granny, dogs, cats and hens. On leaving his previous career as a children's nurse Gary worked for over ten years supporting others towards achieving their life goals, rediscovering their confidence, mastering their motivation, being creatively confident and enjoying the lives they truly deserve. Gary's paintings very simply reflect his love of - and strong sense of kinship with - nature. They reflect the little moments of everyday magick that nature shares when you least expect it.

Wendy Andrew – Wendy has painted and drawn since she was very young. She went to life-drawing classes with her professional artist father from the age of six and she attained a degree in fine art at Cheltenham in 1979. Her beautiful wildlife paintings have been internationally reproduced as cards, jigsaw puzzles, trays, kitchenware, tins, collectors plates etc. Gradually Wendy's love of The Goddess, mythology and the 'old ways' found expression in her work. Over the last few years Wendy has become internationally recognized for her exquisite Goddess and mythological paintings. Her paintings are in collections worldwide.

Wendy's paintings can be seen reproduced as prints and cards as well as in various publications including 'Wicca and Witchcraft' magazine, 'The Pagan Wheel', 'Spirit and Destiny', 'The Bardic Handbook' by Kevan Manwaring published by Gothic Image, 'The Personality Profiler' by Claire Gordon published by Carroll & Brown Ltd, 'Fairies 101' by Doreen Virtue published by Hay House, and 'Pentacle' magazine Summer 2007. Also in Doreen Virtue's Goddess oracle cards and Unicorn oracle cards.

annie b. – Annie b. (illustrator) lives in Cornwall with her husband and son, and it is here she has developed her own unique style and language, in oils, watercolours and chalk pastels, creating art from the heart for wellbeing as well as running Art from the Heart Workshops using guided meditation to help people connect to their hearts and creativity. More details of Annie b.'s artwork and options to buy originals, prints and cards please visit http://www.annieb-art.co.uk . Annie b. says:
"My aim is to create artwork that helps us all feel love and joy, see the bigger picture and the natural flow of life so that we all may dance in harmony together, be mindful of mother earth and each other, and know the Divine Oneness we truly are."

Rose Blakeley – I have always had a very lively imagination, which has drawn me into the many realms of fantasy as a writer and artist. It is my writing that leads me with the greatest strength, and as the words manifest they entice me into another world where I become infused with the essence of their meaning. That place has never deserted me and although the route to its source is endless, it is very often the exquisite magic of nature that takes me there first.

Rosalie Bottley – A chance meeting in London and there she was surrounded by beautiful paintings. Rosalie shines bright in a world that looks drab in comparison. And it is with considerable gratitude that her glorious and vibrant work features on the cover of this book. **www.facebook.com/rbottley**

Mia Bradbury – Having always felt a strong connection to nature and mythical legends of our ancient past, Mia grew up searching out the special places, feeling most at home in ancient woodlands and stone circles. She takes her inspiration from the natural world, mythology and the awe inspiring presence of the sky. The pull of the moon, the rise and fall of the seasons, and the turning of the stars. Her art is a way of connecting with the magic that is all around us and within us. **www.mia-bradbury. co.uk**

Christine Burnett – My work is based on a love of texture, layers and the beautiful world of nature.
I try to reflect this in the pieces I create through the use of stitch, collage, scraps of words, hints of hidden things. My current influences are Cas Holmes and Anne Kelly, both textile artists whose work I really respect. (I recently attended a workshop with Anne Kelly and have two pieces of my textile work represented in her RSPB show in Sussex).

Maria Forrester ~ I'm an Illustrator based in the West Midlands and my work is inspired by the history of witchcraft, pagan practice, nature, myths, legends and fairytales. I live in a semi-rural location where I am in tune with nature, the wheel of the year and the Goddess. I have always had a strong bond with animals which also feature in my work.

I mainly work in acrylic paint. Texture is important to me so I enjoy experimenting with graphite rubbings which brings out the inner child in me. I visit graveyards, stone circles, and woodland, and also collect items that create interesting patterns to include in my work. I love the unexpected results this method employs and the subconscious images that appear by working in this way. www.mariaforrester.co.uk mariaillustrator.blogspot.com

Jan Fowler ~ My work is inspired by magic, nature and the Goddess as Earth Mother. My current work is a celebration of the divine feminine in all it's aspects, an empowerment of womanhood. I live in Norfolk where I am working to encourage women to explore their own power and creativity.

Alexi Francis ~ I live in Brighton UK. It's great being beside the sea, but I would love to live in the country to be close to nature, to wakeI live in Brighton but long to live somewhere wilder. I am an artist/illustrator inspired by nature and mystery, myth and story. Long ago I studied zoology and a love of nature and wildlife has been present all my life. A few years ago I spent a week on Havergate Island off the Suffolk coast where I spent much time watching birds and hares. The hares fascinated me in particular, hiding out amongst the thrift and gorse with their wild, amber eyes. It was a magical, memorable time. www.alexifrancisillustrations.co.uk

Erica Hemming ~ I do most of my creative dreaming in a rainbow hammock at the bottom of my garden. My "hand-made" life is a patchwork of themes supported by my love of the Past and Ancient Cultures, Middle Eastern derived Dance forms and a Nature-centred Spirituality. My images are illustrative, colourful, and influenced by Dreams and Folktales, Nature, a word or a phrase, or trying to capture a stunning moment in time. People often respond to my work by saying that I have helped them to recognise the Inner Spirit or Beauty of the Ordinary. My philosophy in craftwork is the reuse and recycling of elements with minimal modification to the state in which I have found them; bringing a new life to objects otherwise discarded as "use-less". In Commissions I am working with including personal symbolism into the images to provide an extra layer of meaning and memory touchstone for the client. www.artsrushandcane.moonfruit.com

Shari Hills ~ Shari's paintings are inspired by the natural world and the creatures that inhabit it. Working from her studio in Cornwall, she uses transparent glazes of watercolour to capture the ethereal, often magical effects of light and colour in nature. Sometimes tissue paper or hand made papers are worked into the paintings to provide depth or texture.
A member of the Drawn to the Valley group of Artists based in the Tamar valley, Shari teaches a variety of watercolour classes/workshops in Cornwall, Devon and Somerset and demonstrates for art groups and societies. www.sharihills.co.uk

Yvonne Hortin ~ Living in the Sunshine Coast of Queensland Yvonne is a registered nurse and midwife as well as a Bard with OBOD. She practices complimentary therapy and her own special brand of energy healing. Her love of all animals, especially cats are a source of inspiration for life and healing. And she walks alongside the Ancestors in a journey of joyful creativity.

Godfrey Lacks - Godfrey lives in Worcestershire with his wife Julie, Julies' Mom Margaret, and two cats, Boswell and Seren. Growing up in the area Godfrey enjoyed from an early age the freedom to roam the local country side, climb trees, jump canals and falling into brooks, engendering an abiding love for nature which has proved formative in his spirituality. The continuing search for expression of that spirituality has lead in recent years to druidry, which has proved embracing and welcoming, and importantly,has opened a long looked for conduit providing some sort of continuity to our indigenous beliefs. Godfrey is a memeber of OBOD, currently exploring the Ovate grade, his interests include making and playing flutes, spending time in nature, and according to Julie, mud! Currently working for local government Godfrey is looking forward to embracing the new horizons of retirement later in 2014, when he intends to get very muddy indeed!

Sam Lauren-Smith - I am inspired by our beautiful countryside and the wildlife within it. Our garden's trees and birds provide infinite inspiration, and I have swapped colour and brush for black ink and pen to tell their stories. Hear them at www.samlaurensmith.co.uk

Steve Madog - Cunning Artes - A swordsmith/blacksmith and psychotherapist exploring the spiritual belief systems and rural folklore of the British Isles. "I create objects that inspire and explore the deeper connections with the unconscious and the world around us. The shear impact of ancient symbolic art and its appreciation is not by chance but by careful suggestions given to the observer purposefully by the artist..."

Having suffered post traumatic stress about 20 years ago I started studying the mind and occultism. I trained for 3 years as a psychotherapist and with Paul McKenna and Richard Bandler. I served an apprenticeship as a swordsmith and continue to acquire new skills to give more expression to my work. Each new skill has added to the media with which I can work. New pieces are often inspired by the skills the craftsmen used and the time period and folk lore attached to them.

Paula McFadyen - Paula McFadyen of Burnt Offerings, is a self taught artist, working in a variety of mediums such as ceramic sculpture, painted pyrography, watercolour and acrylic. Paula draws her inspiration from her love of animals and the magical landscape of the Scottish Borders, where she lives. She has dedicated her life to the Goddess and her art is a re-flection of the spiritual path that she follows. Paula formerly devised self help and recovery courses for a national charity. She is also a life coach and healer and is currently writing a book on spiritual recovery.

Anna Newberry - Anna is intensely spiritual and deeply connected to the creative pulse that ripples through our land. With her pagan soul she reaches out to others, her mantra is that 'love' will heal the world and she shows this in everything she does. Apart from pole dance and baking, sugarcraft and tea, her greatest love is her rats. Anna describes herself as a 25 year old pagan still trying to find her path in life, but learning from the journey?

Lisa O'Malley - Dip into the world of magic and mystery and there you will find the wonderful artistry of Lisa O'Malley. Her paintings sing the old stories with love and joy. Find her on www.facebook.com/lisa.omalley.1426

Hare Light © Sam Lauren Smith

Poppy Palin - Poppy is the author of nine previous published books and a contributor to two others. These include the Waking the Wild Spirit Tarot (Llewellyn 2001) Craft of the Wild Witch (Llewellyn 2004) Spiritwalking (O-Books 2006) and Wild Spirituality (2012). Poppy has been a professional tattoo artist, a teacher of English and Head of Art in a London school. She's an illustrator who's worked for magazines and illustrated two of Rae Beth's successful Hedge Witch series. She's also an artist, soul-poet and singer whose life is devoted to the wild-spirited way: an imaginative, individualistic approach to expressing our innate – and utterly untamed – spiritual impulse. Her next project's are the second edition of The Greening (edited and improved) and her brand new Everyday Tarot deck/book set.
www.poppypalin.org or contact her via email **poppypalin@gypsymoondesign.fsnet.co.uk**

Yvonne Ryves - Yvonne Ryves is the author of 'Web of Life' published by Moon Books as part of their Shaman Pathways Series. Yvonne writes a monthly blog for Moon Books under the title of 'Shaman Corner'. She is a regular contributor to Indie Shaman Magazine and has also had articles published by Cygnus Books, Natural Connections, Watkins Review and Earth Star Magazine.

Yvonne lives in West Cork, Ireland where she works as a Shamanic Healer, Reiki Master, Chios Energy Master/Teacher, Past Life Regression Therapist and Australian Bush Flower Essence Advanced Practitioner. She runs workshops and courses on a variety of aspects of energy healing and shamanic work including Reiki, Chios, Munay-Ki, Shamanic Journeying, Pendulum Dowsing and self-development. Yvonne holds a Certificate in Counselling, a Teaching Certificate, a BA and MSc in Education. She is currently studying as a Bard with the OBOD. **www.yvonneryves.com**

Stuart Taylor - Stuart Taylor combines organic farming and conservation on his farm in North Wales. He is a member of local writing groups ID Books and Cross Border Poets. His path includes Druidry and Yoga.

Tiana - I have been truly blessed to have the position of Head of Art and Artist in Residence at a wonderful school nestled in the shires. I work alongside young men aged 11 to 16, who share between them a wide range of emotional, behavioural and social difficulties, though, it would be perhaps more accurate to say that it is they who teach me.

My role within this community includes theraputic art and spirituality through art as well as 'sessions' for individuals who are in crisis. Outside of school hours, I quietly run small groups and arty workshops as well as offer my services as a channnel and it is this 'gift from source' that informs both my group work and art.

Tiana has produced a number of books amongst them, Goddess Within and Crow Messengers also act as companions to her wonderful Oracle sets.

Hennie van Geel - I am a Dutch man, married, father to three adult sons, grandfather to two grandchildren. All my life a Pagan, member of OBOD since 2006. Somehow Arthur, Wales, Brittany, Scotland, Cornwall, Ireland and of course England, have always been pulling at me. Oh, yes, and Dragons. However over last year much of my time has gone into Faerie. So, in short, I am a reasonably lucky Bard. Some of my poems can be found at **sites.google.com/site/henniespoems**

Mary Walton - With a love of painting, sculpting, mediation and her garden Mary says this is a personal journey with the artist as sherpa. She says 'My spirituality has taken me abroad and back home again and I still have many miles to go. Watch this space'. marywalton@fsmail.net

Sharon Zak - I am a writer, artist, healer, catalyst, counsellor and spiritual guide. I grew up with a powerful Earth-focused spirituality and I remain deeply connected to the land. I follow Druidic teachings as well as the ancient guidance I am gifted. I reach out heart-to-heart for I am in service and part of that service is to help forge the connections we so badly need.

I co-founded Slippery Jacks with my wonderful husband Dave and our aim is to make spiritual work available with an ethos of non-exploitation. **www.slipperyjacks.com; www.sacredgrove.co.uk**

Raising awareness and funds for the Hare Preservation Trust

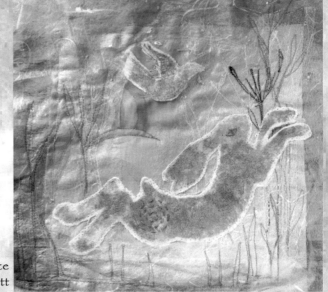

Called to Dance
© Christine Burnett